THE DEATH OF MUSIC JOURNALISM

Simon Sweetman ❯

to Katy, for everything that you are
for Oscar, to all that you will be

Cover image by Matthew Couper.
Cover design by Sarah Bolland.
Typesetting by Paul Stewart.
Edited by Paul Stewart and Mary McCallum.
Author photo by David Thomsen.

A catalogue record for this book is available from the National Library of New Zealand. Kei te pātengi raraunga o Te Puna Mātauranga o Aotearoa te whakarārangi o tēnei pukapuka.

ISBN 978-1-98-859527-6

Printed in Aotearoa New Zealand by Wakefields Digital.

BOOSTED the arts foundation

Published with the support of
Boosted and the Arts Foundation Future Fund

THE CUBA PRESS
Box 9321, Wellington 6141
Aotearoa New Zealand

CONTENTS

Starts off well, a lot of name-dropping though ... and I don't hear a single

The (difficult) second section

Starts off well, a lot of name-dropping though ... and I don't hear a single

Simon Sweetman, this is your life

I was thinking
about how
one time we
couldn't afford
the bills in the flat
– a guy had drawn up
a charter, he'd even used
the word 'vestiges' –
and there was a flat meeting
because I was dragging
the chain.

the power was going
to be disconnected, the
internet, in its infancy,
would no longer slow-crawl
at all.

and it was up to me.

time to be a hero.

that's how I saw it.

actually, time to just
pay the bills.

I had to sell some of my
CDs. I sat in my room.
I chose ten – of several hundred.

I felt disgusted.
Went down to the lounge, for a break.

And a drink.
I lit a smoke (so dramatic!)

Thought long and hard about the next
things to go – the symphonic hits
of Phil Collins was an easy choice, so was
The Very Best of Elvis Costello
(I had all the albums is all, no need
for that compilation too.)

But what else could go?

Sure, there was a bunch of CDs by
obscure '80s jazz drummers.

There was that Brendan Power one –
his harmonica classics sounded like rubbing
your tummy and patting your head, but it
wasn't the sort of magic-trick you
needed to listen to often.

I softened when I returned, started
chucking out Frank Zappa-this and
Beach Boys-that. Dolly Parton,
Guns n' Roses too (tit for tat).

I took the CDs – and a squash racket,
an old robot, some books, a hockey
stick, various other things
to Cash Converters.
It didn't convert to very much cash.
I took them straight back.

And down the road – to
the second-hand stores.

First time for me. I didn't
think I'd be back.

I thought I had to build
a collection – I didn't seem
to be thinking too hard about contingencies

for how to listen to
the collection if I couldn't
pay the power bill. But still …

I thought you had to have it all, every
album – the good and the bad. The terrible,
the silly, the magical, the miserable.
And then a guy in a shop told me that
a collection was like a garden, it would
only bloom after a good prune.

I looked at him like he was Shakespeare,
Rimbaud, Baudelaire – Fuck, I didn't care,
I thought it was so profound.

The power bill got paid and plenty of
other CDs stayed in my room.

Some I listened to, some were lined
up (almost straight away) for the next cull.

Can you imagine
a time when music was currency.
When you could pay your bills by
selling your CDs.

Years on, I sold four crates
of records – no issue.
Did it in a heartbeat.
My son's – in fact.

That'll get you realising
what's important.

You better have the fucking
power on – and all the other
shit that doesn't
matter better be out of the way.

I took a photo of Sam Hunt in Upper Hutt 20 years ago

I have a photograph of
Sam Hunt. I took it looking
up at him from the floor.
My jaw down by my camera,
and me in awe of it all.

It was about 20 years ago and
I had been reading his words for
at least 10 years then – I had met
him briefly outside the pub in
Hastings where he was looking
to cadge a fag after reciting Baxter
and quoting lines from Dylan, Lou Reed
and Keith Richards.

I told him – in nervous-schoolboy-rising
voice – that I loved Lou Reed and knew
the New York album he'd referenced, my
favourite. I hadn't had to tell him I snuck into
the pub underage – and when he asked me
for a durry I was almost embarrassed to be
a healthy non-smoker.

He signed my book, *Simon, from one*
Lou Reed man to another, Sam
and I could only ever read it in his voice – like
a poem only he might ever write.
I loaned that book out to someone many years
later – never got it back.

A year after taking this photograph of
Sam shaking the poems from his shoulders
I was his opening act. Nervously I read a
poem about how 'history' and 'opinion'
were both seven-letter words, but only
one fits correctly into the crossword – and
this was inspired by the cross words
me and my wife had been having
as she focused on completing
the newspaper puzzle, and I
became Sermon Sweetman –
going on about how Elvis really
was the best, the greatest, the first, the one.

After my set there was a note at the bar
to join Sam in his room – and I did. He had
a bottle of wine he wanted to share, said
he didn't like hanging in the bar for too long
during other people reading because he'd
get bugged by the punters and it wasn't
fair, to him, or the person onstage or
the others in the pub there to listen.
We drank the wine and he told me
he had seen a couple of my poems
and I'd done a good job – and he liked
very much the one about
the crossword. I told him, far too quickly,
that he could have it and shuffled through
the pages to hand him that poem.

He nodded and several seconds later
declared, 'Well, alright!' He stood
in the stovepipes and opened
a little vintage suitcase. Mumbling
as he showed me his kid's school photo
(he carried it in the case with him, it
was the whole class photo, covered in

Gladwrap, and his son's five-year-old face
was circled in red marker) he said something
like, 'Well, you've given me some of
your very best words – I'd like to give you
some good words too …' He shuffled through
typed pages and then paused to look
at one a while. Then loudly said, 'Yeah.
Yeah. I'd like to give you some Wordsworth' –
as he handed me a cover-poem
which made total sense since the sum worth
of his own words is forever held in his head.
I kept that Wordsworth poem
in a folder for years – then lost it
or binned it or loaned it out like the signed book,
never to return.

I've got the photograph still.
I look at it most days.

Mark Knopfler called my house one time

Mark Knopfler
called my house
one time.

(Okay, okay, it was a
planned interview – but
still. Knopfler handles them
himself, schedules it. Then *he
calls you.*)
He said, 'It's Mark here,
is this Simon?'
'Yeah, hi, Mark,' I said. I'd been sitting
at my kitchen table on a Friday night,
waiting for the call, nervous,
off to a gig straight after.
'This is Simon. How's things?'
And then he said very little, suggesting
we crack into it.
(We cracked into it.)

He had a new album to plug – it was,
like many of his solo albums, immaculate
and nearly unremarkable, profound in its
polish with the highlights being
extraordinary, but too long …

and once we'd covered the essential
tick-the-box stuff about the writing
and the recording of the new album

we talked about his old band
and how they'd never reform

and he pitched his philosophy
around songwriting:

'You've got to get behind
the plough.'
Do the work.

Do the work.
That's what he was
saying. That's what
he – in fact – at one
point even said.

I got to ask him about
Tina Turner's song Private
Dancer. He wrote it – she
recorded it, most of
Dire Straits is on it
but not Mark Knopfler.

'A scheduling conflict,'
he started, almost bored by
himself. But he
has his killer line in waiting,

'I would have done
it but I was on the other side
of the world – doing something
else, they couldn't
wait – so they gave Jeff Beck
a call and he came in
and laid down the world's
second-ugliest guitar
solo …'
I knew time was running out
and I had to lob in a final
question – was it to be about
his brother, and what I assumed
was animosity?

But just then the nagging of
Well, what is the Ugliest Guitar
Solo in the World? crept into
my mind. I started thinking about
whether Twistin' By The Pool
or Walk Of Life had horrible
guitar solos (because they are
horrible songs).

But as I went to ask it the intro
to Brothers In Arms started playing
in my mind, the stinging Strat lines
from Telegraph Road echoed, that
evocative intro from the live version
of Once Upon A Time In The West
circled too. And so many solos,
including, yes, of course, Sultans
Of Swing. It was all merging
and I panicked and muttered
something about his
brother …

'Well, I would answer that,
Simon,' Mark said. Then
paused. Timing, his masterstroke,
in concert, on record … and
in interviews too …
'But I've already given
you five minutes extra
beyond the allocation. So
we'll leave it there. I enjoyed
the chat – have a pleasant
rest of the evening, won't you?'
I didn't.

I jumped straight
into a cab to get to
a show and sat watching a really
boring gig – a mess of
wannabe-supergroup
action – racking my
brain about the world's
ugliest guitar solo – all
the while knowing his
line was just a line.

The fucking problem

Anita O'Day
didn't know
she was being
filmed for
Jazz on a Summer's Day.

Have you seen
that fucking film?
It's everything.

And then right
in the middle of
everything

Anita O'Day
shuffle-saunters to
the stage.

She has this hat.
And gloves.
The dress.
And so much sass.

She was high as
a motherfucking kite.

And she sings one
of the greatest versions
of one of the greatest
songs.

Sweet Georgia Brown.

And she's on the junk,
and unaware of the cameras
and it goes down in history,
goes down as history.

She was just trying to
make it through the set.

And yet, I'm supposed
to say that some flavour
of whatever month is good

just because they have
a lot of 'likes' on Facebook,

followers on Twitter
and some towering – and
unrealistic – version of
the latest kind
of self-belief.

This is the
fucking problem.

'All you can do
is learn
to be
a good loser' –

you know who
said that? You can guess
I'm sure, because the
end of the poem is
nearly here.

Anita O'Day said that.
Everything she said counted.

Whether it was for
the record

or not.

Meeting Bruno

When I was 17,
it was a very
good year.

I met Bruno Lawrence
in the most perfect
Kiwi way.

I was packing my
drum kit into the back
of my car

When I heard a
sandpaper-voice say,
'Flash drums, cunt,'

then a huge belch.
I looked back to find
New Zealand's finest

actor and one of
our greatest drummers,
there in rugby shorts,

a T-shirt and
jandals, nursing
a Steinlager.

He told me
to come to his
house sometime

to get a case for
my cymbals.
I never did.

I wish I had.
About a year later
he was dead.

Boxing on

I was never
much of a
flirt …
and might only
have ever had one
go at it.
The girl was talking
to everyone about
all sorts
of things –
and everyone
was interested.
I heard her
say that some
band had a
photo of her
stomach that they
took on tour.
It was stuck to one
of the drum cases.
I pushed a couple
of more sensible suitors
aside to attempt
my move, saying,
'That's such a coincidence.
I play the drums and I once
got my stomach
stuck in one of my
drum cases.' I think
that was me flirting …
I never saw her
again, can't remember
her name

and the story about getting
my gut stuck – was made
up. I mean I had
the stomach – a keepsake
I'm stuck with – but I never
owned road cases
for my drums, only some
old boxes to fill up
with stories.

A ham sandwich walks into a bar ...

The old joke has it
that if Karen Carpenter and
Mama Cass had
just shared the same
ham sandwich
they'd both
be alive today.

It's hilarious – because one of them
was rather thin, the other not so much.

they both died due to conditions of
the heart.

(I've no idea where the ham sandwich
rumour came from, but people love
to talk about Cass Elliott choking
on this food-type – essentially just
a comedy-prop – in bed. Why this is
funny and how this came to be any sort
of public knowledge is beyond me.)

Look, there are parallels:

They were both incredible. Huge
talents. The star of the show in their
respective groups. With voices that
take you away, that make
your heart break.

They broke their own hearts,
busted, beyond repair.

Karen died of anorexia nervosa.
Cass died from a heart attack.

Let's make a joke about these
amazing women. Let's sell short
their legacy by having a laugh.

Let's talk of ham sandwiches, they're
always funny. Ham, bacon or pork.
It all comes from a pig.

Let's laugh at what these women did,
reduce them down to an ugly – and weird
and frankly baffling punchline.

Because to think, instead, of
Dream A Little Dream and We've
Only Just Begun and the 40
or 50 other great recordings
between them – at least –

is harder to do, less of an
easy laugh, than making up
a story about a ham sandwich
in bed.

Also, how would Cass Elliott
saving half of that bread
and pig, back in 1974,
do much
for a first-peak-of-fame
Karen Carpenter,
nearly a decade before she
lost her battle?

Jokes about ham sandwiches
are a shortcut to actually
thinking.

I know this because
I just googled: *Ham Sandwich Jokes*.

There are 32 different ham
sandwich jokes on one website.
Though to call them *different* is
awarding entirely too many points
for originality.
For the most part they are
variations on the same things:

You can buy a ham sandwich for a
fiver, get a fancier one for a bit more
or get a handjob for about $200. These
are the three options listed on the menu
in the bar where this joke is about
to take place.

The guy in the bar calls out, 'Who
gives the handjobs?'
The (blonde) barmaid says
(with a smile) that she does the tug.

'Well,' comes the punchline, punching up
and punching down and punching all around,
'Wash your hands and make me a ham sandwich!'
There's another about a guy that is upset

he always gets a ham sandwich for
lunch. He says if his wife gives him one
more he'll jump off the building at the
construction site where this joke takes place.

The next day his wife gives him more pig
in bread. And he leaps to his death.
His workmate had promised much
the same if he got another peanut butter.

At their funeral – because they had one together,
for no real known reason – their wives discussed
the situation. Peanut Butter Wife reveals her husband
actually packed his own lunch every day.

So that's deeply hilarious.
The other main kind of ham sandwich joke has a
ham sandwich walking into a bar and the barman
(blond or not, we are never told) points out that,
'Hey, we don't serve ham sandwiches here!'

'That's okay,' says the sandwich.
'I just want a drink.'

That'll be soggy bread almost instantly, I'll bet!

Did these incredibly witty and wise stories
of bread and ham and the combination
of the two to make a meal-sized snack
arrive on the back of waiting a decade
to mock the deaths of two brilliant singers?
Or were they doing the rounds already?

I'll never know.
But I can't say,

after 600 words or so,
that I don't really care.

32 jokes about ham sandwiches.

(Fuck me, that's outrageous.)
And – *cue* Twilight Zone *music*

Mama Cass was 32 when she didn't eat
any part of a ham sandwich and was
in fact already asleep, dying before
waking, late in the night and late in
July 1974.

Just under ten years of waiting
and plotting, and planning the
perfect weight-mocking food-prop
joke …

And early in the morning, after making
it through the night, a poorly Karen Carpenter
cannot take another step. Her frail body,
her damaged soul, her illness in control,
its final ravaging, creeping down the spine …

she collapses on the floor of her parents'
bedroom. She's unable to sign the divorce
papers as planned. She's unable to breathe.
To sing. To play the drums. To do anything.
She dies in February. It's 1983. And she
was 32.

Friends just can't be found

Here's the key thing about
Bridge Over Troubled Water:
when Paul Simon wrote it – he had
just two verses. He took it to
Art Garfunkel and asked what he
thought. Artie told him to go away
and write a third verse – told him he
had half a good song but it needed
finishing.

Paul returned with
that triumphant sailing on bit
i.e. *The Whole Fucking Journey
of the Song* –

and he decided it would ease
his mind if Garfunkel took the
lead and sang the hell out of it
– sending this white, modern
gospel hymn to the heavens.

That's fucking teamwork right there.
Two guys that grew to hate one another
but respected the shit out of each other all
the while. They had professional acumen
and admired it in each other – they had separate
strengths. Art Garfunkel's voice is honey and
heaven, but it's fire too. Soul fire. He was
more than just a lead singer, and more
than just an ethereal harmony vocalist, more
than a conjurer – he was also
an arranger, a conceptualist, a motivator.

Paul Simon knew enough to know that he
had done all he needed to do with this song

in the writing. He would hand it over. He would
sit it out. Play a background role, let Artie take it
up the charts and send it to live on
in various places, in the spaces in hearts
around the world over decades and forever.

I saw Simon & Garfunkel twice in 2009.
Two nights in a row. First night I was up
the front – fourth row. Unbelievable.
Second night I was right down
the back – for a different perspective.
I'd already seen Art Garfunkel solo.
A few years on I'd see Paul Simon
with his incredible band.

Two interesting things happened
the nights I saw Simon & Garfunkel.
They each did solo sets
in the middle of the show. And Paul
really seemed to come alive
when he got to parade on a few
of his own musicians and bask
in the world-fusion stew of pop and
folk songs married to
South American and African rhythms.
It was as if he could shake off
the cape of nostalgia.

Art Garfunkel's solo set felt like
admitting defeat. As if suddenly he was
judged on the merit of
the material alone and it really wasn't
up to much apart from
Bright Eyes still melting hearts.

But the incredible moment happened on the first night.

There was a microphone malfunction.

Art Garfunkel didn't notice. So he
kept singing – but nothing came out.
We could hear him – just. Because
we were close enough. But there was
no chance for the room to hear
those magical words. So the audience
instinctively joined in.

The song – of course – was Bridge Over Troubled Water.

So you had this audience joining in to lend a hand.

Our time had come

There we were. Right behind …

And standing behind Art Garfunkel, as he
thought he was battling on, was Paul Simon.
Benevolent gift-giver of songs (to Artie and us).
He was smiling. And Paul hardly ever smiles.
He was gracious and he was blown away actually.
He wiped a tear from his eye.

Some 40 years after
he'd written the song
he saw a whole new meaning
come from it. He saw and heard
a new spirit lift it.

One of my favourite things to watch –
and I mean this, I watch it
most weeks – is Art Garfunkel and
Paul Simon on *Saturday Night Live* in 1975.
They had just recorded
My Little Town together and released it twice,
on their respective solo albums of the time.
They are co-musical guests on *SNL* – they are
playing The Boxer and other
Simon & Garfunkel classics. It's their
first televised reunion.

They are sitting together
on stools, an adoring crowd
in the studio and at home.

And what does Paul say
to this old friend? To the guy
that helped shape his songs
and give them wings …

'So, Artie, you've come crawling back?'
Pain is all around. The promise
to supply comfort long gone.
A bridge too far.

Weary, feeling small.

Friends. When you lose them,
both of you have to know –
that friendships just can't be found.

Beatles theory

A lot of people
seem to think
that Paul McCartney and John Lennon
hated each other – were competitive,
and that Yoko was a pesky nuisance as well.
The Yoko thing? That's mostly racism.
And sexism too.

Paul and John are on the record
as having had a bit of hang-time through
the '70s, a spectacularly awful drunken jam –
a night where they watched *SNL*
together, thought about going to the studio
to claim the joke-cheque ($3000
or whatever it was) that Lorne Michaels
held aloft, but just got high instead.

John and Paul would fire some barbs at
one another or get the press to
do it on their behalf.

But they also visited and talked and thought – often
– about recording together again …
John heard *McCartney II* – or at least heard
Coming Up. He pulled to the side of the road.
Loved it. Said something like, 'Paul's Back!'

John would be back too. Soon. He'd be
'starting over' – the sadness of course
was that was number one with a bullet …

But the real thing no one talks about
is how George and Ringo kinda grew
to hate Paul the most.

And I know why.

And here's the theory.

They were the ones that Paul
could do without. He could replace them.
He could at the least approximate them.

They knew it. Kinda. He knew it. Certainly.

He played drums on some Beatles tracks –
Dear Prudence and Back In The USSR
are good starters. He played some killer
lead guitar too – fucking Taxman, mate.

Fucking owning it!
He had, more than once, told George
and Ringo how to play their parts.
He came up with suggestions, arrangements,
and it drove them crazy.

And then when they were all cast
as Professional Beatles in the docos,
you could sometimes see
they were seething.

Paul struts in like David Brent
or Noel Edmonds, doing a dance with the camera.
Says, 'Allo, Georgey-boy, ma love.'
And tousles his hair to remind him – even
in his fifties, he's still and always
two years younger.

George grimaces through the hug, shrugs,
says, 'I didn't know they
made vegetarian leather jackets.'

In another scene, Ringo is tapping
on his knees as Paul and George
mug it up on the ukes. Ringo says
that he just likes hanging out.

He's got his pals. Prior to this
he was not-doing-coke-anymore
with the Fat Controller.

He's heartfelt, he fucking means it.
Paul talks over him. Makes a gag.
(Makes George gag.)

Now Lennon was a rough-as-shit guitarist,
but he had something when he'd hit
at those strings. The baggage. The grit. A cynicism.
And such wit. He was a wife-beater, he even
hid that inside a song. He tried a few mea culpas.
And far too many margaritas. He was
a drunk. He was hurting. He was
a child for far too long.

But he was punk-as-fuck. And he was –
when it suited – the leader of the band.

Paul never forgot that.

Just as Ringo and George
never forgot that Paul,
bless him – *bless him*, a genius,
the greatest melodicist, a jobbing writer
to put all others to shame –
had told them they were
not only nothing, they
were something he could do himself.

They smiled for the photos, threw peace
signs – Ringo's doing it still. But I reckon
there's more than one reason he always
wears sunglasses.
And George went to his grave never
turning up at a McCartney jam.

Convalescence

Brian Eno listening
to a harp album

convalescing. he can
barely lift a finger.

the taxi-cab banged him up
pretty good –

or pretty bad, depends
how you look at it.

the album
of harp music on

in the background. the rain
takes over – or it provides

further soundtrack, depends
how you hear it.

he has no control
over the volume

he's just regaining
control of himself.

his mind is free
to wander.

so it does. and from this
state, and in

this state, he
creates Ambient

Music, without
even lifting

a finger. *because he couldn't*
even lift a finger.

Everyone

I said
the orchestra
was bad

and a guy
wrote in and
called me

a cunt
and told
me to wash.

We're all critics
at the end
of the day.

All hail

Sure, I could point to almost any other Prince album before it and a few after it as being 'better' – but the sentimental favourite will always be Prince's soundtrack to *Batman*; not the actual score and basically the soundtrack to the movie of *Batman* that was playing in Prince's head. Prince the star. Of course. It's actually one of his best albums-as-snapshot. It's concise, it's song-based. It showcases pop, funk, ballads – there's just enough indulgence and weirdness to remind you it's Prince and not just somebody trying to be Prince. And more than just about any other record in my collection this one anchors me to a time and place. I remember going to see the film for a second time, in Napier. My parents picked me up afterwards. Me and a friend. Not quite teenagers. We made them put the Prince soundtrack tape in the car for the drive back. Bungy-jumping had just made it to Hawke's Bay so we had to take a detour. I remember the car stereo was pumping Electric Chair. And we made it to the car park of Countdown where, for $25, you could bungy-jump from a crane over the shingle car park. No scenery – but there was a double air-bed mattress ready to save any Partymen and/or Partywomen. We watched one Partywoman rip her black T-shirt off and go down in her off-white bra. She looked as filthy as her bra (the perpetual reason for its off-whiteness). She poked her tongue out and shrieked. She made the sign of the horns with her hands. Her hair: the stuff you hate to have to fish out of a communal plug-hole. She is framed for all time, in a slow-motion fug of her own cigarette smoke. The car stereo playing The Arms Of Orion. She was in that instant beautiful. Worth thinking about the next time we shuffled the deck of Batman bubblegum cards. The heat rising up off the tarmac and bubbling away at the corners of the photograph in my mind. Hawke's Bay, you rotten egg. You beautiful, mad, bad thing.

Giving the drummer some

I met Steve Gadd.
He had
played on many of
the greatest songs ever.
And just in case
he'd forgotten
I reminded him.

I got him to sign
my records.
He was embarrassed –

and told me he liked
the fact that I was wearing
shorts.

It takes all sorts. And I was the
only one he'd seen not wearing
long pants. So that was a talking
point.

A local drummer-ape had been assigned
as his driver. When he wasn't sitting
on Steve Gadd's knee
he was picking the lice from his back and
swallowing swiftly as if it contained the
secret to the feather-touch triplet movement between
the hi-hat, the bass drum, the snare.

I didn't dare tell Mr Steve Gadd
that I was sure I could play 50 Ways long
before I could.

But as he looked at me with the eyes that had stared
at the back of Paul Simon's head

I could tell that he knew I would not
have it right.

What's left to say?
I told him that Late In The Evening was
some sort of secret pathway.

He told me he liked my hat.

A day later I would drive 200 kilometres
to give him a hat – oh, and
to watch his gig.

I was blown away to see and hear
the guy that I had been aware of since
I was seven or eight.
His shuffle-feel intros, outros
and bridging fills for Paul and Carly Simon,
for James Taylor and Steely Dan,
for Chick Corea and others, all dangled
around him like dazzlers and chains.

He was blown away to see me
in jandals – 'You're wearing flip-flops?'
he questioned – in the voice
that had told Rickie Lee Jones
he 'might have something'
for that bit during Chuck E's In Love.
The local drummer-turned-chauffeur
was crouched on the stage, later in
that evening, almost sitting
inside the pocket of the solo
to Aja.

Ready to pounce
at the drop of said hat.

Tight connection (to the heart)

our souls
can see
what we can't
hear

Bob Dylan
and Joan Baez
at the microphone
together – his song
shared by them, long
after the flame
has died

their souls
can't see
what we can
hear

The (difficult) second section

End of the Larkin Line

When the first Traveling Wilburys album was released we took a drive into Hastings – Friday night, late night shopping … it was me and my brother in the back of the car (our usual spots) and Mum and Dad up front. They bought the album – on cassette tape. No CDs then – not in our house anyway. And so we drove in, got told on the way that the folks would be buying an 'important' album. And then, when home, we all sat on the floor by the stereo – and they played it. Mum and Dad told us about how this was one of The Beatles, and the guy from ELO, and that Roy Orbison was a rock'n'roll legend. And Bob Dylan a poet and a prophet. Tom Petty was the young guy – the new kid on the block. But he'd been around the block riding on a tune or two … we sat and listened to the album right through. And then again – a second time straight away. We were allowed to stay up late to take it all in (or try, at least).

Your mum and dad might fuck you up but the real tragedy is you hardly ever remember to thank them.

Father and Son

Part 1

I hardly ever
think of Cat Stevens
– but when I do, I instantly
think of *one thing*. And it is not
a particular album or song. It is
not any one greatest hits
compilation. It is not the
fact that it was the soundtrack
to any drive
along the Napier–Taupō road
for my high school years.
And it is not even the university chum
who was convinced that Cat Stevens
was a paedophile because
of his penchant for writing songs like
(Remember The Days Of) The Old School Yard
and Where Do The Children Play?
Those are not the things
I *instantly* think of. I instantly
think of one *situation*
whenever Cat Stevens plays.

My father used to play
the *Greatest Hits* in the
car, relentlessly, and in an effort
to engage with him on this
subject, 13-year-old Me said,
'This is a good CD. I particularly like
the song Father and Son.'
(This would later turn
up on the university
chum's list of suspect-songs too.)

The car arrived home
with us in it. The way it
usually did. And
13-year-old Me figured
the throwaway conversation
was over. So I got out
of the car and went inside.
My father stayed in
the car.

I was in my room later that
night doing homework.
And my father arrived
saying, 'That song you
mentioned earlier … I think
you were trying to tell
me something.'
'Yeah I was,' I said. 'I was
trying to say that I liked
that song.' 'It's probably my
favourite on the album. And
so that's why I said that to you.'
But my father looked at me
as if I had basically started
singing the younger man's verse
in the song, aiming it right at him.

Actually I was about to
ask him what year
Norman Kirk died in office. But
he was busy preparing his
look, adjusting his head as if he
was about to sing his reply.

The 13-year-old Me struggled
to convince him it was just a
good song. And in the process of
doing that I fell instantly out of
love with it. Never to have
any interest in it ever again.

The curse being I would play in
a covers band on and off for
about three years – *that* song
was part of the nightly repertoire.

My mum told me that
the reason I got out of the
car and Dad stayed in the
car that night was because
he sat and listened to
the song three times to
try to understand what he
thought was being said
to him.

Part II

When the old man had
his best mate in town –
guy who'd played
drums in his band

well, suddenly everything
I'd ever done with music:
every radio appearance, every
interview, and those pesky

review controversies
were all up for grabs.
Topics for conversation.
Pride too.

It was all 'Remember when …'
and 'What about that time …'
and 'Didn't you also speak to …'
and 'You saw them, didn't you …'

Not sure if I was meant to be
more than bemused.
But it certainly didn't matter, that
night that the rent was due

and that there had never been
a plan. It was bragging rights time.
And 'Play it again, son!'
This time with feeling!

Why depression isn't just something that happens to other people

there's an army of
shadows following
us all

you only crash into
the wall if you
admit to seeing them

Date scone

We lined up at the
counter, to order
coffees and a snack.

The way families do
when catching up now.

My mum and my
dad, visiting
briefly, and we

had done a wee
tour of the town – so it
was time to sit down
for a bit.

My father ordered
a date scone – and when
the person at the counter
asked if he'd like it heated
he threw that heat right back:

'Absolutely not!'
We found a table
and he was still going …

'Absolutely pointless!'
No one said anything. A beat.
Another. And then,

'I hate when they ask
if you'd like the scone
heated. Who wants a
scone heated? It ruins it.
Simple as that.'
These
were the
facts.

I made the mistake
of suggesting
that – actually – maybe
more than a few people
liked their scones
heated. Seemed likely
if the wait staff figured
it worth asking of anyone,
right?

'Well, I don't.'
A beat. And another.
And then:

'It ruins the flavour –
There's no point –
It's messy –
The butter turns to slop –
It crumbles. It falls to
bits. And pieces –'
These were the reasons.
Or some of them.
My mother was stirring
her drink.

I was too.

(Well, stirring my own
drink, I mean.)

The scone arrived.

I felt like it deserved
a fanfare, I heard trumpets
in my own head at least.

He spread the
butter, corners,
a thick blanket,

yellow on yellow,
but faded. A quick
flick of the knife,
turn it over and
spread once again.

And then the
first bite.

We waited. We felt
we needed to.

'See,' he announced
proudly. 'That. Is. A.
Scone.'
I didn't check with
Mum – but I was sure
we'd both known that
already.

'And that,' he continued,
'is how you do it. You
don't heat it. There's
no point. It's ridiculous.'

I said, 'I agree,' and
he looked hopeful for
a second.
'It's certainly ridiculous,'
I confirmed,
as we stood to head
for the car.

new lovesong

i'd sink to my
knees if i didn't
have you
i should sink
to my knees
because i do

Big O/little o

Only in dreams will
I hear a voice like
the Big O.
I wake up to my own
little o telling me
it's time to make
his lunch.
It's a far cry –
so blue.

The flat on The Terrace

i walk along the
terrace, see the flat
i lived in for years

and years.

i had no cares, back
then, beyond knowing
where the next CD
was going to come from.

my flatmates thought
i was mad.

and these were people that
cheated on their girlfriends,
took carving knives with them
for late-night walks – you know,
just in case.

one of them tried to kill
a mouse by smearing peanut
butter on a golf-putting-return-machine,

one of them drank cups of
tea while shitting,

one of them watched
pornos while doing
his taxes.

i wanted to shout, 'and *i'm*
the bad guy,' like michael
douglas does in that film. (hang on,
maybe i hadn't quite seen that, just
then.)

it was madness though. that's
for fucking sure. no one carried a
key and one day when the window
wasn't unlatched, for someone to

open and step through,
he just threw his drink bottle
through it, pushed the glass
aside – and stepped in …

… no problem?

when it was my
night to cook – i'd write
a cheque for the pizza place

and disappear. go elsewhere.
anywhere else.

(possibly in a bunker, because
the cheque would likely bounce.)

i had a room full of music
and cigarette smoke, a head
full of – possibly – undiagnosed
anxiety (or more likely laziness)

and i had about 50 or 60 square-grid
maths books that i wrote poems in.

(the others in the flat could not
handle that.)

the time when i found a guy

taking a piss into an electric
frying-pan on my bed seemed
reasonable – particularly when he
explained that the drinking game in
the other room had it that no one

was allowed to urinate. several of
the others had pissed themselves in front
of each other, probably mid-swig,

but this guy had standards … and a
contingency

and this wasn't even the worst thing
that could happen of a night.

we rode a shopping trolley down the
stairs and into the wall, missing a giant
window that could have launched at least one
of us into a waiting hospital bed,

we drank a five-litre bottle of whisky on a
pouring frame in one night.

someone got laid out for denying
a shot.

and all of this, and so much more
comes flooding back to me, on
wednesdays, after lunch, having
finished one job to get to another

and then from there down the road

to collect my son from his school.

i look across the road at the house –
somehow still standing – and think of tom waits
and bukowski and teaching drum lessons
in the lounge,
while my protesting flatmate
tried to watch tv at the same time.
his arms folded, his brow knotted.

i think of baxter and sam hunt
and lauris edmond and the one-night-stand

that was referred to as a spear-chucker,
presumably because of the colour of her skin.

and that any of these sins don't come close to
the very worst of the behaviour back then.

i heard one of the guys
is a merchant banker – well, why
not, he was rehearsing for that gig
when he was sleep-walking blind-drunk to shit
on a couch.

the other two, i have no idea.

commerce degrees.

and they graduated long before me.

we're all lucky to be alive.

and beyond that, to not know anything

much about each other anymore.

A fine thing

You with your
funny ways,
me with the

things I say.
We're a pair.
And just as

well.
I'd be lost
without you.

You'd probably
get by without
me.

But you'd never
say that. At least
not out loud.

You've always
been a kinder
soul.

That's part of
how the balance
is achieved.

I like to think
that's me doing
my bit.

Or you allowing
me the chance.
A fine thing.

Poems

I never
knew if
my mum

ever read
my poems.

last weekend
we caught
up

briefly.

she couldn't
remember the
name of the

book she'd been
reading, nor the
author – but

she definitely had
it – somewhere –
on her kindle.

'you'd like
her,'
she said.
'she writes
all her
stories a bit
like you
do,
in funny,
long
columns …'

Memory

When my
grandma phoned
I knew something
was up – could tell
by her voice.

She sounded worried.
(And she never worried.)
She asked for Dad's
number; she'd forgotten it,
wanted to call him – needed
to call.

I gave her the number and
then she said, 'Thanks. It's
your grandfather, you see.
I think he's dead.'
And that was it
at the end of the line.

We all drove down.
The man from the
car yard gave us all
a hug, told us to be
strong, that we'd all
need to be together.

And we went to the house.
He was on the bed.
(He was dead.)
He must have known
something was (about to be)
up. He had gone to town,
paid all the bills, mowed
the lawn, and then

had a wee rest. (He's having
it still.)

This was as close to showing
love as he ever got.

All the jobs done.

I was 16, in the middle
of my School C exams.

(I'd have something to
write about the next day!)

They told me to stay
in the lounge, so I didn't
see the body.

But I wanted to see
the body.

I snuck a peek.
He looked calm.

But it also looked
like he wasn't
there. He'd already
left.

I'm glad
I got to see
him that
final time.

No arguing,
no finger pointing,
no hands flailing.

Just a big sleep.

My grandma
sang some old
Scout songs

as they carried him
out of the house they'd
lived in forever.

What was left of
him went out

in a big ol' zip-up
black bag.

Weekend fun

Saturday morning, the kid in bed.
I'm telling stories of the things I did

when I was his age, silly stuff that he'll
laugh at and repeat – and then he'll ask

me to repeat it so he can get
the exact wording and copy my voice.

*

Saturday afternoon, we're watching a film.
Pause, rewind, watch the funny bit again.

And again – and again, and then wait
for more funny bits … expectantly. Hopeful.

*

Saturday night, it's time for bed.
A great day of laughs, no stress – only fun.

One more long cuddle, his legs and body seem
to almost run the length of mine.

He'll be asleep soon and I can worry only then
about all of the time we might never have.

Quick fix

My dad rang
to say they were
on their way
down to fix the dryer door.

He'd found a new one for
only a hundred bucks and
he'd finished all his other
jobs so the four-hour drive
to stay the night was a good
way to fill in a Monday,
they'd bring tea as well …

They arrived when
they did. Him and my
mum. They unloaded the
truck – a ritual. The bag
with condiments and avocados,
limes and lemons, some baking
too.

And then we got down to the
laundry to lift the dryer down.
And clean the area. And sort
the mess.

Then the big reveal:

'Just give us a hand with the
door please, it's down in the truck.'
How heavy could a new dryer door be?

And yes. Of course. A brand-new clothes dryer
is lifted off the truck. A bargain, apparently.
And in it goes.

We show love in some funny ways in
my family.

They left, after
an evening spent watching
YouTube clips of Alan Partridge,
a glass of red and then time for bed.

And now the only thing damp
in the house is the wee bit
around my eye sockets.

Taxi

he's in the back of the
car, as usual, and i'm
his taxi driver.
my son asks me
if the day he was born
was the best day of
my life.
and i say, 'yes.
of course.'
'what about when
you and mum got
married?'
'second. nearly as good.
can't have one without the
other.'
he nods. and i didn't go on
to tell him that the third best day
of my life was when he had
just turned two. we were
driving to hawke's bay
for christmas, he and his
mother asleep.
and i had the ipod connected
to the car stereo. and i'd made
a playlist.
the theme from the tv show *taxi*
on a loop (so that i didn't have to
keep pressing play or find
the repeat function –
i had the same track loaded
30 or 40 times ...)
bob james's perfect fender rhodes
instrumental – with
ralph macdonald on percussion and

idris muhammad on drums. sounds like
eric gale's guitar slow-burning in the
lava-lamp glow.
i was their taxi driver. i'd look
to the left, then to the back-left,
that music from my childhood guiding
the way.
it was like i was the yellow-cab in a time-loop
(a new york minute?) driving over (and over)
the queensboro bridge.
checking my buckled passengers.
seven o'clock.
and
nine o'clock.
resting. their beautiful
faces. those wondrous souls.
all fire. all glitter and gold.
first and second.
(first equal of course!)
and the music my mantra, my
meditation, taking me back to the
friday nights when we'd wait
for dad to come home with the
fish'n'chips, when we'd laugh
at louie's anger and jim's madness
and the weird and silly and wonderful
latka …
me and my brother and my
mum and dad were maybe
at our closest watching *m*a*s*h* and *family
ties, blackadder, the young ones, cheers,
married with children* (and a few others).
definitely *taxi*
but here i was …
driving the white lines with this
music that was taking me back

and taking me back as i was edging
ever-forward … in the yellow-cab of my
imagination. whimsy. nostalgia.
and so much more than that.
(does there need to be more than that
though? those two things are so
beautiful, so joyous and sad all at once,
they've helped me along in so many ways
through so many ways …)
profound beauty all wrapped
up in that slick and lovely groove.
people would maybe call a song
like that 'soulless' – to me it's the very
embodiment of soul …
and so it rolled on and on
and i did too.
checking their faces. me
elated. the calmest i'd been
in an age. or more.
and i was never
bobby wheeler.
i was their alex reiger.
but i was better than alex reiger.
because they didn't just
have me. i had them.
and we had the music.
even if it was only me listening.
that was the third best day
of my life.
and if i whispered that
it was the best,
well, that was only
because they were
asleep.
and i
was their taxi.

Yeah, but that's just, like,
your opinion, man!

The TED Bundy talks

They asked Ted Bundy, after he was
caught, why he was able to strangle and
murder so many people – 17 women at
that point, or something.
His answer: 'There are so many people …'

My question: Who is *they?*

Ted Bundy died in 1989. He is listed on Wikipedia as
an 'American serial killer, kidnapper, rapist, burglar
and necrophile' – just as, say, Lenny Henry
gets the Wiki treatment and is dubbed
a 'British stand-up comedian, actor, singer, writer
and television presenter'.

You can click on hyperlinked text to find out more
about the roles of serial killer, kidnapper,
rapist, burglar *and* necrophile.
Wikipedia assumes you don't need to know
anything else about the roles of actor, singer, writer,
television presenter – nor British stand-up comedian.

There are no further links.

The pro-wrestler King Kong Bundy
was named after King Kong and Ted Bundy.
His aim was to be seen as being
as scary as both, a dreaded combination.

The pro-wrestler King Kong Bundy
is still alive. (This surprised me.) He turned 60.
Just yesterday. (But only if you're reading this today.)

Ted Bundy was regarded as handsome
and charismatic, according to his victims.

I'm not sure how we know this.
We can't quite take their word for it.

I'm sure he did.

Sometimes Ted Bundy kept parts of a victim
for months. Turning a light on, opening
a cupboard, taking some joy from
seeing what was there. From knowing
it belonged – now – to him.

Other times he would sneak into a room
and just bludgeon someone – in the dark.
Smash their skull and leave.

Ted Bundy referred to himself as
'the most cold-hearted son of a bitch
you'll ever meet'.
I never got to meet him.
But I believed him.

In 1989 Ted Bundy died.
He was executed. The electric chair
was his final resting place.

In 1989 my favourite song
was Electric Chair
by Prince.

Winner, winner, chicken dinner!

I am from Hawke's
Bay, where we're
good at the weather.
The best. World class.
Don't believe me?
Ask my dad!
I made that mistake
only yesterday in fact.
Didn't even realise it
at the time,
he asked what I was doing …
'It's hot,' I explained. 'Real
hot. Down here. So
hot right now.'
But it was hot where he was, perhaps
even hotter.
I wasn't competing.
At least not that
I knew.
And though neither of
us could be in two
places at once, and both of
us seemed happy right
where we were,
he had won
the weather again.
Of that he
was certain.
The red ribbon again.
Burning hot.
YES!

Name-drop ... what a cock!

The night we launched
the book
we went out for a bit
of a feed after, and more
drinks – not too many, mind.
I had a big interview the next day.
And a mate of mine – with
experience talking to camera and
interviewing everyone – told
me I really needed
to get
my beauty-sleep

(despite having
the perfect
face for
radio).

'It's only
Kim Hill ...'

I said in return.

The table laughed, well,
all that were sat at it.

And then someone panicked
a bit,
on my behalf,

'Oh no, what if she fucking
just goes at you?'
'I'm talking about
a book,' I said. Calm. Never
ever cool – but fairly collected.

'It's not like I'm on there to
defend fracking – more a case of
talking up Pink Frost. Easy! Right?'
At any rate, that was my last drink.

And it was time to call time
on the night.

Up, early-*ish*, and off
to the station,
I met Kim Hill.
She was nice. Polite.
She bounded around from
the desk to shake my
hand. Eye contact. Warm.
Friendly. Inviting.

I'd figured she might have
been hermetically sealed.

It was fine.

We talked about
the book and some songs
and they played bits of music

and there was one bit where
she had a go at me for being
mean about bands.

But they were shit bands.
And that's pretty much what
I said.

Did Kim Hill really want to
be the one to defend SIX60?

(I didn't think so …)

And then, at the end

of the interview, just as the off-air
light went on, or the on-air light went
off …

and we were thumbing through
music bios and talking about

the then-new books by Pete Townshend
and Keith Richards and one about
Mick Jagger, another about someone
else. I forget now

but then, just like that, Kim Hill,
winner of international broadcaster awards,

said, simply, as if a full sentence, answer and question
problem and solution:

'Mick Jagger's cock!'
It hung there.

(Er, those words, at least.)

'Is it a large one …'
Her famous eyebrow arched,

'… or is it quite small?'
I wished I'd known how to defend
fracking all of a sudden.

'Well,' I said, 'there's a couple of
schools of thought on that one, according
to the books …'

I had to let *that* hang there. I couldn't summon
the strength to ask Kim Hill what she thought.
She told me, anyway. She said,

'Pete Townshend was RATHER IMPRESSED.'

And the other eyebrow, this time, did the little
dance, shimmied in time with the rise of her
inflection.

'But Keith Richards, not so.'
The eyebrow drooped.

It was almost as if I could see the words
doing a little pirouette as they left her mouth.
A bow, or curtsy, to follow.

The hardest part, and you'll
pardon that pun, was Mick Jagger's
cock.

The rest of the interview
had been
easy.

Which is what I said
when I texted my
told-you-so to
Paddy Gower
straight after.

The fluffer to the devil's advocate

All this
cancel-culture,
I don't know.

That's the wrong
end of the stick
as I see it.

I want my cultural
heroes to be
of questionable

morals and ethics. I want
them focusing their
energies on their work.

Being the best at
the art they pursue,
and possibly even the

worst human beings
as either a direct result
of the focus

going into one area and
the balance not being
achieved – or simply

because there's an
evil in their soul.
It's good to have

heroes who are also
villains – for all
they've achieved

you have the chance
to feel superior
on some, important, level.

Mindfulness at heart

the mind
has a heart
of its own

the heart
don't mind
at all

this is
the problem
for all of us

but
could it be
the solution?

Different fires

I thought I
had the
cure for
boredom.

I used to set
the coffee table
alight.

And dance around
its flames. No way
could I be tamed.

Now I know that
boredom
is the cure.

In turn

I'm very good
at talking myself
out of jobs.
That should
actually be
my next job.
I wonder if they
need someone capable
of talking themselves
out of jobs …
And what value
that could bring?
And what the
hours are?
And whether you need
previous experience?
Anyway, I wouldn't
be good enough at it.
It probably doesn't
pay.

John Quatrain

– – – – – – – – – –
– – – – – – – – – –
– – – – – – – – – –
– – – – – – – – – –

A Love Supreme
A Love Supreme
A Love Supreme
A Love Supreme

– – – – – – – – – –
– – – – – – – – – –
– – – – – – – – – –
– – – – – – – – – –

Quatrain refrain

She asks for an end to the music, a chance to rest her head.
A curse of bombardment. I understand – follow her to bed.
There we lie – in truth, in happiness, for all our sins.
My head on her heart. Resting. I swear I hear this
as the place where all music begins.

where all music begins …

where all music begins …

(where all music begins …

where all music begins …)

It takes time to heal but time is not a healer

No, I am not
a healer,
I'm too self-centric.

Wounds bring
words.
And I need the material.

&
in the end ...

Let me entertain you

I got an
email from Robbie
Williams once.
It was to apologise for
the time he shared a picture
of me and my kid to his
2.59 million followers on Twitter.
He wrote *Simon Sweetman –*
Baby Eater (in the tweet, not in the
apology-email; that would be a rank
apology-email, nearly as bad as some
of his music … nearly …)
It was a saga for a bit. And I still get
asked about it a lot.

And basically Robbie Williams
was rather upset that someone didn't
like his show – you would think he'd
be used to it or wouldn't care.

He made bank after that gig. Big time
no doubt. I had to wait six weeks for
about $60 to trickle into my account (after
tax) for the review that got him so upset.

And yet, a year later he was still thinking
about it. He was still getting asked questions
about it. Interviews for his new album were
being taken up with questions about his 'beef'
with the (beefy) Kiwi blogger …

And so I reckon his label or management – or
both – got annoyed and told him he had
to try to make amends …

So, one night, late, after midnight
even, I got this random Facebook

message from a person that worked for his label in the UK.

She asked me for an email address. Told me that RW would be making contact.

Sure, I said. And fired off my deets.

And waited. Although wasn't really waiting … was just living … getting on with whatever …

and then a day or two later, an email from a manager, saying that he would be forwarding a sincere apology from RW to me.

Forwarding because RW did not want to be entering into a dialogue.

Okay, I replied.
And so a day or two after that the email arrived/was forwarded.

Robbie Williams wrote that he was sorry, he said he'd read a piece I had written about the impacts his tweet had had on my family. (There was, for a bit, international media interest. And I knew it would die down in a day or two – and it did. Well, it took a week, I s'pose.)

And so the email said that his heart
sank and he wanted to speak
from one dad to another,
because in that moment, that's
what we were, you see. Just two dads.

Not a thin-skinned millionaire pop star
and an underpaid freelancer.

We were two dads, mate. Just doing the do, mate.
We were so similar, you know. We both had kids, like.
And that meant we were both on the level.
His tweet had been a bad move, that's
what he said. It was, he told me, *just like*
when I have too much Ambien and decide
to go shopping on Amazon – you
know, mate, a bad move. A bit of a dick-move, like.
A silly thing to have gone through with, ya know …

I read it. Thought about hitting delete. Thought
about hitting 'forward' and sending it to whoever …
(But who, actually?
Who could fucking really care, right?)

So I left it. (It's probably in my inbox still.)

A day later the manager sent me
another message. Did I get the message.
I said that yes I did.
I wrote, in fact: *Yeah, got it. Ta.*

And that ended up, another year on,
in the Robbie Williams memoir. His second.
I'm named. My wife is named. My son is named.
We're there over a page or two (or three).

I bet his advance didn't take six weeks to trickle
in. I bet it was worth more than $60.
(Taxed or otherwise.)

His ghost-writer reckoned I was a real tough nut.
A bad guy. Staunch. Tough. Hard to crack.
A jerk of some kind.

Hey. I'm not saying he's wrong.

I know all this because someone
who recently unfriended me on Facebook
sent me photos of the pages of the memoir
as he was reading it.

I am almost through with freelancing.
(Almost.)

There's not a lot
of protection.
Or love ...

Oh fuck ...
Here we go again.

That second Eric Clapton concert I went to

We were
at an Eric Clapton
concert – i.e. *A White*
Room – none more white
when it comes to the blues
and there was a bit of
argy-bargy going on. Some
dude was pushing another
dude and then my dad got all
up in the grill of someone –
chest puffed out – and I'd
never seen that before.
So I had to join in too. I was
worried about the old man,
didn't want to see him go
down like that. Sconed in the
face. Clocked while ol' Slowhand
was playing Wonderful Tonight.

So next thing I'm up
in the face of a guy too.
Don't know what I'm going
to do. But I'm there. To
protect the old man.

To see if I can let my size
suggest I might have packed
a fight. But I have never thrown
a punch – and by any look at me
I'm far better at packing a lunch.

Anyway, the gig was a fucking
blinder! And how the hell did
that happen? EC gave it all away in
about 1970 or at least '72.
He phoned it in for years – fucking

years, absolutely years. Got good again,
for a bit, in about 1990. Which was the first
time me and the old man found ourselves
at an Eric Clapton show.

But this was nearly 20 years on from then.
And ol' Slowhand was very nearly Old Sock and
most certainly old hat. And then, when anyone
least expected it, a vital show – five songs from
the bloody Layla album. His final triumph.

So this was a good save and I put it down
to the clean shave. No neck-beard. Just a few
cum-face guitar solos. And he was the third
best axe onstage at his own show that night.
Derek Trucks and Doyle Bramhall II
owned the show.

Just like my dad reckons he owned the guy
who was trying to own the guy over some
White Boy Blues matter, some drunken-dumb
natter. And I stepped up because I thought I'd
give misguided arrogance a go.

And it's a shame to now place this
as any kind of boast but I play the
elegant-bluff like it's my own
final passage from Layla.
Further on up the road … as the people
filed out from the clinic they were sad
not to have heard Tears in Heaven.

These heathen-cunt-losers.
These jerks. These sopping, sodden fucks.

My dad was basically shadow-boxing, punch
drunk. Owning the streets, planning
a song in his head. His own blues swimming
in the red.

True Stories

my dad and my brother
have this story.

they were driving in
my car.

they were listening to
a tape I had left in –

some Talking Heads greatest
hits-type thing.   and just then,

they drove past the cemetery
and my dad pointed and nodded,

referencing his father's final
nap.   and just as he pointed,

and just as he said
whatever he did about his dad,

the tape, which had 'finished',
sprang back into life

a conversation between me
and my grandfather.

two new talking heads, talking
aloud and maybe saying nothing

much, talking about an old life.
my school project had been

to sit with my grandfather across
several days and document

his life.   he wasn't unwell, we
didn't then know that he had limited

days left on his count.   the clock
ticking, his ticker not so much, not as

well as it had.   and now,
a year or two on from there, or four, or

five, or whatever it was, my father and
brother turned white as, well, ghosts

to hear this voice   just as they
drove past the burial ground.

we were talking about the '60s
(i can remember my father telling me

not to ask his father about that particular
decade, 'he wouldn't have a clue, he was

not good then, didn't understand the '60s
at all.' i don't think my dad understood that

was exactly why I wanted to talk
to his dad about that particular decade.)

two talking heads, prattling on,
same as it ever was.

two garden-variety 'experts', nattering
and solving and pontificating,

teacher. and student.   and we
eventually found our audience

(we had a tape. they wanted to play)
a year or two, or three or four or five on.

the less said about it the better.
we were making it up as we went along.

We bonded over Sonny Rollins and Faith No More and Lenny Kravitz and so much more

for Hamish

We lost a good one this week, a soldier
no longer reporting for duty –

his war over, he wore it as well as he
could, I guess. If you asked me to take

a guess on who might succumb (and how
fucking gross and dumb) I might just have

stammered his name. But that doesn't mean
that it wasn't a shock, hasn't knocked me for six –

doesn't sting more than just a bit. Suicide is
hardly talked about. Talked about hardly.

Speculation isn't wise, isn't nice, is never fun,
shouldn't be done. And confirmation makes you wince.

*

You had a unique energy – you were firecracker mad,
may your dance continue. I hope you paint your masterpiece.

My brother and me

my brother lives in
a different city.
in fact we're
worlds apart.

there are a few years
between us,
and salary brackets
too.

we have different hobbies.
he likes counting his money.
i wouldn't last long
at that.

my brother lives
in a different city.
in fact we're
worlds apart.

but, recently, we've found
common ground. we're fathers.
we have our own families
now.

and we take them to the zoo.
do things, like that.
things people with families
might do.

so on a recent trip, together,
to the zoo – it was a stroll
down memory lane.
we hadn't been there

in that same place, together, in over
30 years. the bears were in different
places, but the further we walked
the more familiar it seemed.

and then we got to the rhino.
majestic thing, its head lowered, and
searching, its horns and hide reminding
us that it is linked to the dinosaurs.

'we're not,' i said, 'leaving
until we see it drop a shit.'
my brother sniggered, not so
much at what i had said,

more at the possibility.
and then, as if on cue,
not a shit, but a huge whooshing
sound, like an outboard motor.

this thing was pissing –
an enormous, efficient surge.
and we laughed.
my brother and me.

no longer worlds apart.
because some days
all you need
is a huge rhino pissing.

Dylan wrote *Infidels* when he was 42

I have
been thinking
a lot about
Infidels just lately,
Bob was about
my age now when he made
it.

That's not worth thinking about
too much –

obviously.

He had made 21 albums
ahead of it though,

so it wasn't a case
of beginner's
luck.

Some people
talk about *Infidels*
like it was a comeback

as if he had ever been
away.

He just went somewhere with
his material that some people
weren't interested in.

That was either their
loss – or it
wasn't –

but it was not
his fault.

He was just doing his
job. as he's always
done.

But *Infidels*
is where he strips
the artifice,

It's where he
aims (right) for
the heart.

Twenty-one albums before it. Many
of them better than albums
anyone else has made.

But on none of those
albums did he ever sum
it up
quite so simply,
so brilliantly,
as when
he said – or possibly
even sung

that he would not handle
it if the person
fell apart on him.
Not on that night.

The yearning of the day just
been, the worry of what might
be to come, and the hope
to have that person not just
then but forever.

A forever that was crystalised
in that moment, that night.

That's the heart of it
all
right there.

Nearly the
best thing
he ever
wrote.

And that's
saying something.

Which is what
Dylan does
almost all
the time.

But mostly
he does it best
when no one's
looking, when
fewer fans
are listening.

That's his secret
gift. He'll never let
the fans see him falling
apart. He knows
they could not
handle it.

He does his falling
apart between the lines.

Saves his best work
for when you need it.

We listen to The Beatles

We listen to
The Beatles
because they're
the best band in
the world – they
mean the most to
the largest number
of people – and
yeah, that's changing
and that's all good
too – but when my
son asks me if this
is a Paul or a John
or a George song, or
tells me that he knows
it's a Paul song because
of the balladry, or a John
song because it's angry,
I can only think back
to when I was his age
and I asked my dad and
my uncle to tell me who the
fourth Beatle was – because
I couldn't remember the name
'George Harrison'.
I was about five years
old, or whatever. John Lennon
had only just died I suppose.
I can't remember if my dad
was sad about that –
but I have to presume
that he was. The world
was, and sometimes
still is, right?

We listen to The Beatles in
the car and on the turntable and
via a Bluetooth speaker. We listen
to The Beatles on the computer, watch
YouTube clips, flip through books.

Will it ever stop?
I fucking hope not.

realtalk

no one ever built a statue
in honour of a critic

but only because they knew
it could never be good enough

Acknowledgements

This book wouldn't exist without me. I think that's fairly obvious. But no book is made by the writer alone. *The Death of Music Journalism* simply wouldn't exist at all without the amazing team at The Cuba Press. Mary, Paul and Sarah have been a delight to work with – so skilled, knowledgeable, passionate, encouraging and open to ideas and collaboration.

A huge thank you to all supporters of this project via the Boosted campaign and my Facebook page. It goes well beyond my wildest dreams to know there is that kind of support.

My wife, son, mother, father and brother are all mentioned in some way in these poems. And they inspired many of them – even if not directly referenced. I hope they are okay with that. I couldn't exist in the way that I do in this world without them. There are so many people I would like to thank and it is when you start naming names that you also start forgetting them.

Matthew Couper, for your friendship and incredible artwork – in general, as well as the glorious cover that makes this book feel alive.

Tony Chad, for being the first person to ever publish my poems. Shout out to Valley Micropress!

Sam Hunt, Gil Scott-Heron, Bill Callahan, John Lillison, Ben Brown, Janet Malcolm, Raymond Carver, Woody Allen, Charles Bukowski, Joni Mitchell, Bob Dylan, Ali Whitelock, Suzanne Vega, Paul Kelly, James Tate, Lou Reed, Willy Vlautin, Sylvie Simmons, Stephen King, Clive James, Joan Didion, Nick Kent, Neil LaBute, Norman Mailer, Tom Waits, Dolly Parton, Tom Wolfe, John Steinbeck, Patti Smith, Steve Braunias, Henry Rollins and Tim Winton are many of the first names I think of when I contemplate writers that put words down in songs or on pages that have smashed me to absolute pieces.

Jim Wilson, Jimmy Jones, Jef Shirtcock, Samuel Charles Herman Walters, Paddy Gower, James Robinson, Carl Shuker, Emily Writes, Pip Adam, Chris Tse, Rachel McAlpine, Freya Daly Sadgrove, Linda Burgess and Katy Robinson have been supportive, encouraging readers and voices I have learned from.

John Coltrane, Bob James, Jeff Beck, Sonny Rollins, Bill Frisell, Cliff Martinez, Clint Mansell, John Carpenter, Keith Jarrett and Wendy Carlos have said more to me than many other musicians. And all without uttering a word.

In recent years Poetry at the Fringe and Poetry in Motion have been supportive environments for me as I've read and road-tested poems in public. Both of these communities exist with great love and support from locals in Wellington and the generosity of spirit and great space that is The Fringe Bar.

Some of the pieces have appeared – reworded, or in earlier versions – on my website *www.offthetracks.co.nz* and my Facebook page.

You can say what you want about these poems … they can't hear you.